LEGENDS OF WOMEN'S TRACK AND FIELD

BY EMMA HUDDLESTON

Book design by Sarah Taplin
Cover design by Sarah Taplin

Photographs ©: Lee Jin-man/AP Images, cover (left), 1 (left), 29; AP Images, cover (right), 1 (right), 10, 15, 16; Jiro Mochizukii/Image of Sport/AP Images, 4; Bettmann/Getty Images, 7; Intercontinetale/AFP/Getty Images, 9; Fred Kaplan/Sports Illustrated/Set Number: X11588 TK1 R7 F25/Getty Images, 13; Eric Risberg/AP Images, 21; Mark J. Terrill/AP Images, 22; Matt Dunham/AP Images, 25; Matt Slocum/AP Images, 26

Press Box Books, an imprint of Press Room Editions.

ISBN
978-1-63494-287-4 (library bound)
978-1-63494-305-5 (paperback)
978-1-63494-341-3 (epub)
978-1-63494-323-9 (hosted ebook)

Library of Congress Control Number: 2020913892

Distributed by North Star Editions, Inc.
2297 Waters Drive
Mendota Heights, MN 55120
www.northstareditions.com

Printed in the United States of America
012021

About the Author

Emma Huddleston lives in Minnesota with her husband. She enjoys writing children's books, running, hiking, and swing dancing. After learning about these legends in women's sports, she hopes young people feel empowered to be the best they can be.

TABLE OF CONTENTS

CHAPTER 1

PIONEERS

Nobody was going to catch Diane Leather. The English runner started fast. She stayed fast. And with one final burst, she crossed the finish line in 4:59.6. On May 29, 1954, Leather became the first woman to run the mile in under five minutes.

Sixty-five years later, Sifan Hassan lined up to run the same distance. Just like Leather, she reached the finish line faster than any woman in history. But by July 2019, runners were much faster.

Sifan Hassan pushes herself to the finish line in record-breaking time.

Hassan, who is from the Netherlands, covered the four laps in 4:12.33.

Track and field is a simple sport. People have taken part in running, jumping, or throwing contests for centuries. Yet the sport is constantly changing. Athletes keep running faster, jumping higher, and throwing farther.

Babe Didrikson was known for doing a little bit of everything. Opportunities for women to play sports were often limited during her lifetime. That never stopped the Texas native. She starred in just about every sport imaginable. But her three Olympic medals came in track and field. In 1932, Didrikson won gold in the javelin throw and the 80-meter hurdles race. She added a silver medal in high jump. She broke world or Olympic records in all three events. Didrikson might have won more medals,

Babe Didrikson clears a hurdle at the 1932 Olympics in Los Angeles.

but women could only compete in three events at the time.

The first modern Olympics were held in 1896. Women were first allowed to compete in track and field in 1928. Still, for years the sport's organizers believed women were too weak to compete in all of the same events as the men. One by one, women proved them wrong.

At the 1948 Olympics, Dutch sprinter Fanny Blankers-Koen left the track a winner time after time. She won the 100- and 200-meter sprints, as well as the 80-meter hurdles. Rules limited female athletes to three individual events. But Blankers-Koen added another gold medal in the 4x100-meter relay. Had she been allowed to compete, she might have won some field events too. After all, she held the world records in high jump and long jump.

Blankers-Koen was nicknamed "the Flying Housewife" for her diverse background. She could fly through the air and around the track. She also was a mother and wife. When she

Fanny Blankers-Koen cruises to the gold medal in the 200-meter sprint at the 1948 London Games.

achieved her historic wins in 1948, she was 30 years old and pregnant with her third child.

CHAPTER 2

BREAKING THROUGH

Twenty-year-old Wilma Rudolph stepped onto the track at the 1960 Summer Olympics in Rome, Italy. People who knew her when she was young may have never guessed she would make it there. Rudolph was stricken with polio as a child. She wore a brace on her left leg. Some people with polio became paralyzed or had weak muscles. But Rudolph had overcome her illness.

Rudolph attended Tennessee State University. The track coach there was

Wilma Rudolph breaks the tape as Team USA wins gold in the 4x100-meter relay at the 1960 Olympics.

Ed Temple. He scheduled practice for his team, the Tigerbelles, three times a day, rain or shine. It was time to find out if that would pay off.

Rudolph waited behind the starting line. As soon as the gun went off, she exploded into a sprint. She did it over and over again in Rome. In the end, she won gold in the 100- and 200-meter races and the 4x100-meter relay. She was the first US woman to win three golds in one Olympics.

Women were making advancements beyond the Olympics as well. On a spring day in Boston in 1966, a figure crouched in the bushes on the side of a road. She wore a black swimsuit, her brother's shorts, and men's shoes. She watched hundreds of men run by in the Boston Marathon. Women weren't allowed to take part in the race. That was about to change.

Bobbi Gibb smiles after becoming the first woman to run the Boston Marathon in 1966.

Bobbi Gibb had been denied entry. At the time, women were presumed to be too weak to run 26.2 miles (42.2 km). But the 23-year-old Gibb was determined prove them wrong.

Suddenly she pushed through the bushes, jumped out, and joined the race. Gibb became the first woman to run the Boston Marathon.

The next year, 20-year-old Kathrine Switzer became the first woman to both register and run the Boston Marathon. She had registered as "KV Switzer." As a result, marathon officials didn't realize they were allowing a woman on the course. In 1972, the race officially began allowing women.

In 1979, Joan Benoit set out to run the Boston Marathon. She had never seen the course. But she had heard of the section called Heartbreak Hill. She knew it would be challenging. Partway through the race, she asked a runner next to her when the hill would come up. He looked at her puzzled. He said they had already run it.

YOUNGEST AND OLDEST WINNER

At 16, East German Ulrike Meyfarth won gold in high jump at the 1972 Olympics. She was the youngest athlete to win gold in a track and field event. Then in 1984, she won Olympic gold again. That made her the oldest athlete to win the Olympic high jump competition and one of two women to win gold 12 years apart.

Joan Benoit is crowned after winning the women's division of the 1983 Boston Marathon.

Benoit finished strong and won the race. Then she won it again in 1983. Her time of 2:22:43 that year was a world record. In 1984, she won gold at the first Olympic women's marathon. Her impressive career led to her induction in the US Olympic Hall of Fame.

CHAPTER 3

TO THE NEXT LEVEL

Zola Budd was a rising star. She had set the 2,000-meter world record in 1984 at age 17. She was also known for running barefoot. But the South African runner was the underdog in the highly anticipated 1984 Olympic 3,000-meter race.

US sensation Mary Decker was the defending world champion at the distance. She started running competitively at age 14. In 1984, at age 23, she was entering her prime. Decker had set world records at six distances, from 800 to 10,000 meters.

Zola Budd, *center*, passes Mary Decker just before their infamous collision.

Plus, she would be competing on a home track. The Olympics were held in Los Angeles.

Decker led the pack early in the race. A little over halfway through, Budd picked up the pace. She got to the front. The runners were close together. Decker's thigh bumped Budd's foot. Budd regained her balance. In a split second, Decker fell. She ripped Budd's number off her back on the way down. Budd kept running as boos came down from the crowd. Some fans thought Budd tripped Decker when she cut into the lead.

Upon hearing boos, Budd purposely slowed down. She was overwhelmed and wanted to avoid attention.

LONG-LASTING SPRINTER

Merlene Ottey has 14 World Championship medals, which is the most of any female sprinter. The Jamaican sprinter specialized in 100- and 200-meter races and relays. Her career lasted from 1978 to 2012. Ottey medaled in five of her seven Olympics.

Decker didn't finish due to a hip injury. Budd finished seventh. Both women continued their running careers afterward. But the historic fall defined them.

There haven't been many people who could compare with Jackie Joyner-Kersee's all-around athletic talent. She was best known for the heptathlon. That tests athletes over seven events. Competitors have to be good at many different skills. A native of East Saint Louis, Illinois, Joyner-Kersee took silver in 1984. Then she won back-to-back gold medals in 1988 and 1992. Her 1988 world record score of 7,291 still stood as of 2020.

What made Joyner-Kersee even more amazing was that she was also the world's best long jumper of her generation. She won three Olympic medals in that event, including gold in 1988. Only one woman in history has jumped farther. In addition to defeating other competitors, Joyner-Kersee achieved all her success while battling asthma.

In 1988, a US sprinter made history in an unforgettably colorful manner. Florence Griffith Joyner was known for her sense of style. The sprinter nicknamed "FloJo" raced in bright, fashionable outfits with long, painted nails.

At the 1988 Summer Olympics in Seoul, South Korea, she showed she was the fastest woman in the world. FloJo set world records in the 100- and 200-meter races in. In 2020, both marks still stood. Her times were 10.49 seconds in the 100 and 21.34 in the 200. Few sprinters have come close to breaking either.

Florence Griffith Joyner sets the world record in the 200-meter semifinal at the 1988 Summer Olympics.

CHAPTER 4

MODERN STARS

Shelly-Ann Fraser was dressed in black, yellow, and green. A massive crowd filled the Olympic stadium. She was at the starting line for the 2008 Summer Olympic 100-meter dash. The gun sounded. Fraser burst out of the blocks. Two Jamaican teammates charged close behind in nearby lanes.

No one could catch Fraser, though. With a time of 10.78 seconds, she became the first Jamaican woman to win the 100. Teammates Sherone Simpson and

Shelly-Ann Fraser reacts after winning gold at the 2008 Summer Games in Beijing, China.

Kerron Stewart tied for second place at 10.98 seconds. Jamaica swept the event.

Fraser was nicknamed the "Pocket Rocket" for her small size and speed. And she had a lot of speed. Fraser won another gold medal in 2012 and a bronze in 2016.

Many of the world's fastest sprinters have come from Jamaica and the United States. In the 200-meter final at the 2012 Olympics, five of the nine women were from those two countries. Fraser was one of two Jamaicans. Allyson Felix was one of three Americans.

Fraser and Felix pulled ahead. They battled it out over the last 50 meters. Felix was victorious with a time of 21.88 seconds. Afterward, she spread her arms wide and held the US flag behind her as photographers from around the world captured her excitement.

Allyson Felix reaches the finish line first at the 200-meter finals in the 2012 London Olympics.

Felix is the most decorated woman in Olympic track and field. She won her fifth and sixth gold medals at the 2016 Olympics. No woman has matched that total. Felix also has three silver medals over her four Olympics. In addition to the 200, she has also won medals in the 400 and relays.

Shot put thrower Valerie Adams was ranked third going into the 2008 Olympics. But with a spin and a grunt, she released a winning throw in Beijing, China. The New Zealander won gold again in 2012 and silver in 2016. At the 2011 World Championships, Adams threw a personal best of 21.24 meters (69 feet 8.25 inches) to win her third of four world titles.

Poland's Anita Wlodarczyk is a legend in the hammer throw. At the 2016 Olympics she won gold and set the world record. But she broke her own record a few weeks later and threw 82.98 meters (272 feet 3 inches). At that time, Wlodarczyk was the only woman to ever throw farther than 80 meters (262 feet 5 inches), and she had thrown that distance or more 11 times.

Valerie Adams competes in the shot put during the 2016 Olympics in Rio de Janeiro, Brazil.

For the 2021 Tokyo Olympics, the track and field program expanded to 23 women's events. Women also compete in several other types of road races and competitions outside the Olympics. They've come a long way from the days of sneaking into marathons to prove their toughness and talent.

NO. 1 IN THE WORLD

US sprinter Sanya Richards-Ross was the best 400-meter sprinter in the world from 2005 to 2009. She won four Olympic gold medals from 2004 to 2012. The first three came in the 4x400-meter relay. Finally, she won the 400 individually in 2012 and regained the No. 1 ranking in the world that year.

Sanya Richards-Ross clinches the 4x400-meter relay gold medal for Team USA in 2012.

MILESTONES

1948
Fanny Blankers-Koen wins four gold medals at the Summer Olympics in London, England.

1972
Faina Melnik of the Soviet Union wins the discus at the Olympics. In April she had become the first woman to surpass the 70-meter (230-foot) mark.

1987
Bulgarian Stefka Kostadinova high jumps 6 feet 10.28 inches (2.09 m) to set the world record, which still stood in 2020.

1988
Jackie Joyner-Kersee sets two world records while winning Olympic gold in the long jump and the heptathlon.

1995
Ukrainian Inessa Kravets sets a world triple jump record with a distance of 50 feet 10.25 inches (15.50 m).

2009
Pole vaulter Yelena Isinbayeva of Russia beats her own world record at 16 feet 7.21 inches (5.06 m). She has 10 of the top 20 all-time highest vaults.

GLOSSARY

asthma
An illness that causes difficulty breathing.

paralyzed
When the brain cannot control body movements.

polio
A disease that can cause nerve damage, paralysis, and sometimes death.

register
To sign up for an event.

sensation
A famous, popular, or accomplished person.

stricken
Having fallen ill.

TO LEARN MORE

To learn more about legendary women's track and field athletes, go to **pressboxbooks.com/AllAccess**. These links are routinely monitored and updated to provide the most current information available.

INDEX